**Grade 4**

C000001767

# Improve your theory!

## Paul Harris

FABER *ff* MUSIC

# Welcome to Grade 4

Here's what you should know as you get going on this book. If there are any gaps, have a look at *Improve Your Theory! Grades 1, 2* and *3* and ask your teacher.
Tick all the things you know (but only if you really do!)

- [ ] These notes and rests:
- [ ] And triplets, too …
- [ ] These time signatures: $\frac{2}{2}$ $\frac{2}{4}$ $\frac{3}{2}$ $\frac{3}{4}$ $\frac{3}{8}$ $\frac{4}{2}$ $\frac{4}{4}$ $\frac{6}{8}$ $\frac{9}{8}$ $\frac{12}{8}$
- [ ] Grouping beats and up-beats in all the above time signatures
- [ ] Treble and bass clefs
- [ ] Bars, bar-lines, the stave and all notes on the stave
- [ ] More than two ledger lines above and below the stave
- [ ] Key signatures and accidentals (sharps, flats and naturals)
- [ ] Constructing major, harmonic and melodic minor scales; tones and semitones
- [ ] Octave transposition
- [ ] C major; G, D, A, E majors (sharp keys); F, B♭, E♭ and A♭ majors (flat ones)
- [ ] A minor; E, B F♯, C♯ minors (sharp keys); D, G, C and F minors (flat ones)
- [ ] Melodic and harmonic intervals, tonic triads
- [ ] Composing simple four-bar rhythms, phrase structure
- [ ] A reasonable number of terms and signs and performance directions!

Put anything you're not sure about in this box and ask your teacher to fill in the gaps before you get going on Stage 1.

# Contents

## A message from Paul Harris

Welcome to *Improve Your Theory! Grade 4*. I very much hope you'll enjoy working through this book and learning about the music that you play or sing. You'll learn about how music is written down and really get to *understand* your pieces and songs. Through knowing theory, you'll play, sing, sight-read and perhaps even make up your own music with much more accuracy and confidence. It will also improve your aural, scales and ability to play expressively. And you'll learn lots of interesting and fun facts about music along the way. Many people think that theory is dreary … it really isn't!

 Audio tracks for the Aural/listening activities are available to download from www.fabermusicstore.com/ImproveYourTheory4

✓ Answer sheets are available to download from www.fabermusicstore.com/ImproveYourTheory4

# Stage 1

## Facts box

| | Simple time | | | Compound time | | |
|---|---|---|---|---|---|---|
| | 𝅗𝅥 | 𝅘𝅥 | 𝅘𝅥𝅮 | 𝅗𝅥. | 𝅘𝅥. | 𝅘𝅥𝅮. |
| Duple | $\frac{2}{2}$ | $\frac{2}{4}$ | $\frac{2}{8}$ | $\frac{6}{4}$ | $\frac{6}{8}$ | $\frac{6}{16}$ |
| Triple | $\frac{3}{2}$ | $\frac{3}{4}$ | $\frac{3}{8}$ | $\frac{9}{4}$ | $\frac{9}{8}$ | $\frac{9}{16}$ |
| Quadruple | $\frac{4}{2}$ | $\frac{4}{4}$ | $\frac{4}{8}$ | $\frac{12}{4}$ | $\frac{12}{8}$ | $\frac{12}{16}$ |

**Reminder!**

**Duple time** = two beats per bar

**Triple time** = three beats per bar

**Quadruple time** = four beats per bar

### A few helpful hints …

● Rhythms should be written in a way that makes each beat clear.

● Group 𝅘𝅥𝅮 𝅘𝅥𝅯 and 𝅘𝅥𝅯 within beats using beams.

● Only use ties where they are needed to make beats clear.

● The same rhythm may be used in different time signatures, but it will look and sound different:

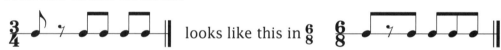 looks like this in $\frac{6}{8}$

Clap these two rhythms, the first while tapping a 𝅘𝅥 pulse and the second while tapping a 𝅘𝅥. pulse.

**1** Insert the correct time signatures at the start of these rhythms.

**2** Complete these sentences:

A 𝅗𝅥. lasts for twice as long as a _____ and half as long as a _____ .

A 𝄾. lasts for _____ as long as a 𝄾.

**3** Rewrite this rhythm, halving all of the note-values. The first note has been given.

**4** Rewrite this melody with the notes grouped correctly into ♩. beats. The opening has been given.

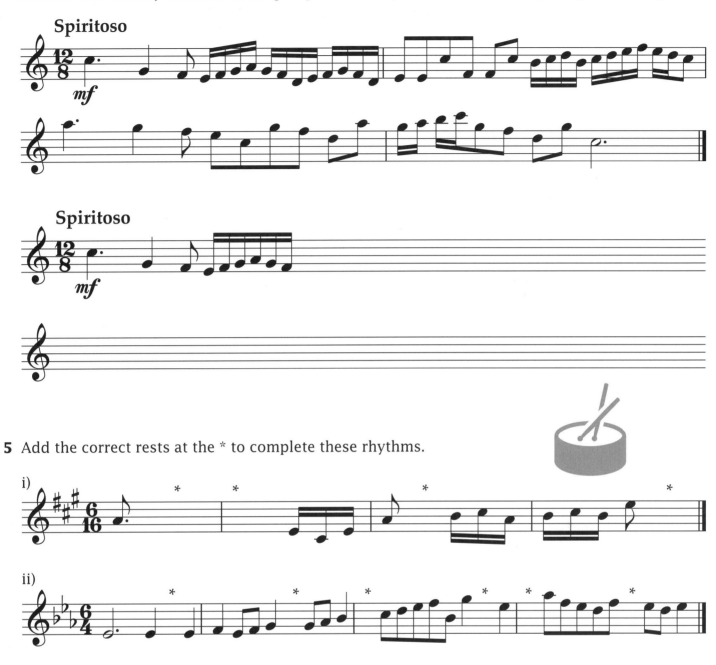

**5** Add the correct rests at the * to complete these rhythms.

**6** Add bar-lines to the following extracts.

**7** Travel through this musical maze, following the route of the correct
time signatures, to reach the destination.

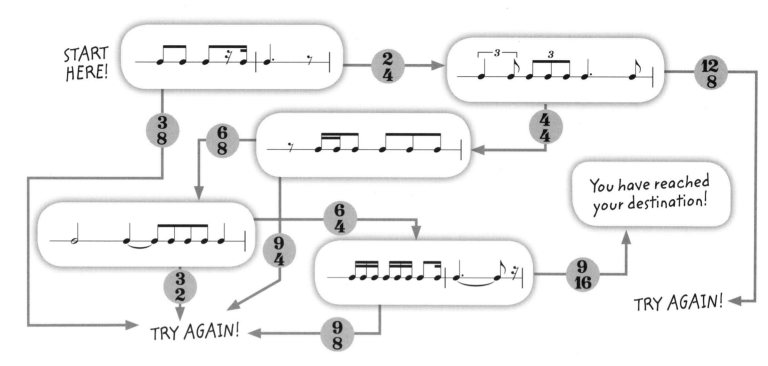

**8** Have a look at this piece. Counting or tapping the pulse, clap the rhythm
and then answer the questions below.

### You never know what's coming around the corner

- Add the correct time signature at the start.
- Think about the character of the music and the tempo you would play it,
  then add an appropriate performance marking at the start.
- Mark the phrases with a ⌐⌐ above the music.
- Which notes will probably sound like a bit of a surprise? Circle them in the music.

  Try to play the piece (or get someone to play it for you) and see if you are right.

- Rewrite the first three bars in 4/4 doubling all the note-values – the opening bar has
  been completed for you.

# Making connections to your pieces

Choose a piece or song you are currently learning that uses interesting rhythms, and write out the first few bars on the staves below.

● What kind of time signature is used (e.g. 'compound duple time')? _____

   Explain the top and bottom numbers. _____

   _____

● What is the key? _____

● In the workspace, write down all of the performance instructions you can find and describe their meaning.

● Rewrite the first two bars of your piece in the workspace, transposing either up or down by one octave and using the most appropriate clef.

### Workspace

---

## More connections

Tap the pulse and clap the rhythm of your tune, then make up your own tune to the rhythm.

## Aural/listening

track 1

Listen to these four short pieces and decide on the time signature from the following:

$\frac{2}{4}$  $\frac{6}{8}$  $\frac{3}{4}$  $\frac{9}{8}$

1) _____    2) _____    3) _____    4) _____

### Theory box of fun

In his ground-breaking book **The Art of Strict Musical Composition** (1776), Johann Kirnberger wrote: '$\frac{4}{4}$ time has a very emphatic and serious motion and is suited to stately choruses, fugues in church pieces, and pieces where pomp and gravity is required, whereas the character of $\frac{3}{4}$ appears to be gentle and noble. But $\frac{3}{8}$ has a liveliness that is somewhat frolicsome.' Do you agree with Johann?

# Stage 2

**New note-values:
breves, double dots
and duplets**

## Facts box

- 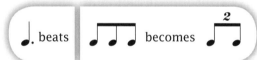 A **breve** is a long note that lasts for two semibreves:

In the time signature of $\frac{4}{2}$, a breve lasts for a complete bar (i.e. for four 𝅗𝅥).

- **Double-dotted notes and rests** are so-called because they are followed by two dots. The second dot adds half again to the length of the first dot:

- **Duplets** occur in compound time, when the dotted beat, which is usually divided into three equal parts, is divided into two instead:

**1** True or false?

‖○‖ = ○ + 𝅗𝅥 + 𝅗𝅥 + 𝅗𝅥    **true / false**

𝅗𝅥.. = ♬♬ + 𝅗𝅥 + ♪.    **true / false**

duplet = 𝅘𝅥 + 𝅘𝅥 + ♫    **true / false**

duplet = ♬ + ♫    **true / false**

**2** Rewrite this $\frac{6}{8}$ rhythm in $\frac{2}{4}$. The first bar has been completed for you.

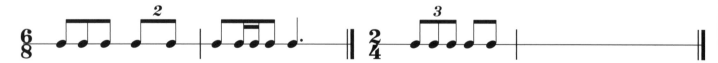

**3** Rewrite this rhythm using notes of half the value. The first note has been given.

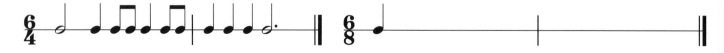

**4** Write the equivalent rest for these notes:

𝅝· =       𝅘𝅥.. =       𝅗𝅥.. =

**5** Join up these rhythms with the correct time signatures and descriptions.

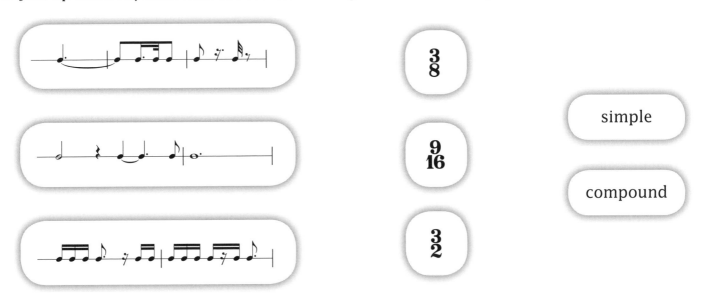

$\frac{3}{8}$

$\frac{9}{16}$

$\frac{3}{2}$

simple

compound

**6** Have a look at this piece, then complete the puzzle questions below.

### Fanfare and stately march of the theory teachers

- The last note is a _____ and lasts for _____ minim beats.

- Add the correct time signature.

- How many semiquavers are there in the first two (tied) notes altogether? _____

- Try to imagine what this piece sounds like in your head, then play it or ask a friend or teacher to play it for you.

- Add an appropriate performance mark at the start.

- 𝅘𝅥 + 𝅘𝅥𝅮 + 𝅘𝅥𝅯 = which of these note-values?

Circle the two examples of this note-value in the piece.

# Making connections to your pieces

Choose a piece or song you are currently learning that is in simple time (ask your teacher to find one for you if you don't have one). Rewrite the first few bars on the staves below in compound time, using duplets where needed.

● What is the shortest note duration used? _____

● What is the key? _____ Circle all the tonic notes in your extract.

● Describe the time signature as: **duple**, **triple** or **quadruple** _____

● Try rewriting the first two bars of your tune below, either doubling or halving the note and rest values. Think carefully about what time signature you will need to use.

Workspace

# More connections

● Choose a piece you are learning that includes ordinary dotted notes. Now play or sing it making the dotted notes double-dotted! How does this change the musical effect?

_____

● Make up your own short fanfare using a mixture of long notes and double-dotted notes.

## Aural/listening

track 2

Listen to these four pieces: two include ordinary dotted notes and the other two, double-dotted notes. Write 'DN' for dotted notes and 'DDN' for the double-dotted ones.

1 _____  2 _____  3 _____  4 _____

## Theory box of fun

The longest known note ever held on a wind or brass instrument was played in Wolverhampton, England, in 2006: a clarinettist kept the note going continuously for one minute and 13.38 seconds. If you are a singer, wind or brass player, what is the longest you can hold a note for? Remember to 'breve'!

# Stage 3

**Facts box**

- The most common clefs are the treble and bass clefs. The **alto clef** (𝄡) is mainly used by the viola, as the range of notes on the alto stave fits with the notes that the viola plays. Sometimes, however, it is also used by the bassoon, cello and trombone, especially if they are playing particularly high notes.

- The alto clef is also known as the **C clef** because the line it is centred on is a C.

- Here is the same melody written in the treble, alto and bass clef; notice the note C in each example:

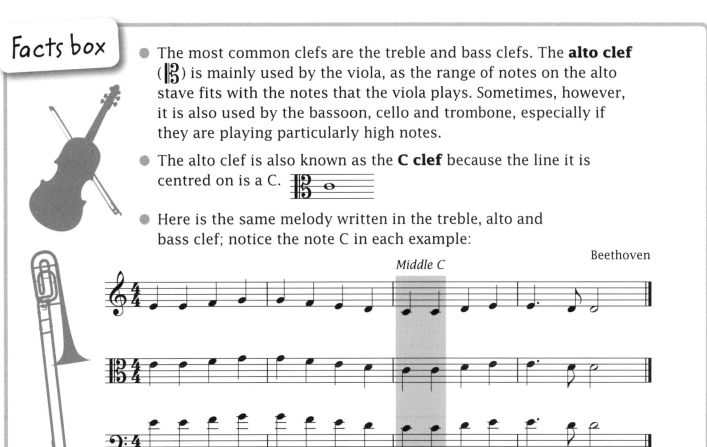

1  Fill in a semibreve on each line and in each space between those given.
   Write the note names underneath.

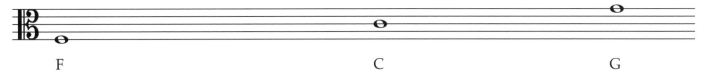

F                                    C                                    G

2  Trace over the simplified alto clef and then draw four more.
   Make sure they are all centred on the middle line (note C).

3  Write out these notes and key signatures in the other two clefs. Make sure you write
   the note out at the same octave as the original (you may need to use ledger lines).

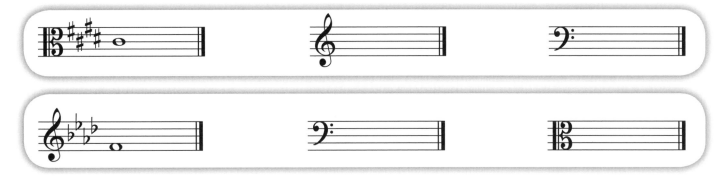

**4** Rewrite the following tunes at the same pitch in the alto clef.

i)

*etc.*

ii)

*etc.*

**5** Have a look at this piece, then complete the questions below.

### I see a C clef

- In what key is this tune? _____
- What is the highest note? _____ What is the lowest? _____
- Circle a bar that includes the key-note (tonic) and then rewrite the bar in the treble clef:

- Why are there only three beats in the final bar? _____
- Which bars include all the notes of the tonic triad? _____

**6** Name these notes and triads.

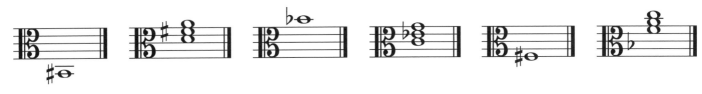

_____    _____    _____    _____    _____    _____

**7** Write out the note names below the stave for the first two bars and
then rewrite the first six bars at the same pitch but in the bass clef
on the staves below. The first bar has been completed for you.

### Two clefs go dancing

Now transpose the first six bars of the melody up one octave
and into the treble clef.

## Making connections to your pieces

Choose a piece or song you are currently learning and write out the
first four bars on the staves below. Make sure you include all of the
information and write clearly and accurately.

- Is your piece: **major** or **minor**? _____

  in **simple time** or **compound time**? _____

- What is the key-note (tonic)? _____
  Circle it in the music and then write it in the alto clef here:

- Write out the first four bars of your piece in the alto clef at the same pitch as the original.

## Workspace

## More connections

- Find and listen to a viola being played online.

- Do you think your piece or song could be played on the viola?　**Yes / No**　*(circle)*

## track 3　Aural/listening

What three instruments can you hear in
these extracts? One of them is a viola!

1 _____

2 _____

3 _____

### Theory box of fun

The **alto clef** is also called the C clef
because it is centred on the note C.
Try designing your own clef symbol
based around another musical letter
of the alphabet!

# Stage 4

**New keys:**
**B and D♭ major;**
**G♯ and B♭ minor**

**Facts box**

**B major** and **G♯ minor** share the same key signature:

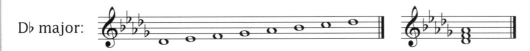

B major:

G♯ minor:
(harmonic)

**D♭ major** and **B♭ minor** share the same key signature:

D♭ major:

B♭ minor:
(harmonic)

> ✗ A **double sharp** raises a note by two semitones. It is needed in G♯ minor to raise the 7th (the F♯ to F✗).
>
> ♭♭ A **double flat** lowers a note by two semitones.
>
> Double sharps and flats are cancelled simply by using a single sharp or flat before the note. ♮ is not needed.

Double sharps and double flats mean that notes sounding at the same pitch can be written in different ways. For example: **C✗ = D = E♭♭**
These notes are called **enharmonics** (see Stage 7).

**1** Using semibreves, write out the scale of D♭ major (ascending) using accidentals instead of a key signature.

**2** Add the necessary accidentals to make this into the scale of G♯ melodic minor.

**3** Write out the scale of B major (ascending) in the alto clef in semibreves. Use the correct key signature.

**4** Follow the clues below and, using the rhythm written above the stave, write out the first phrase of a well-known melody.

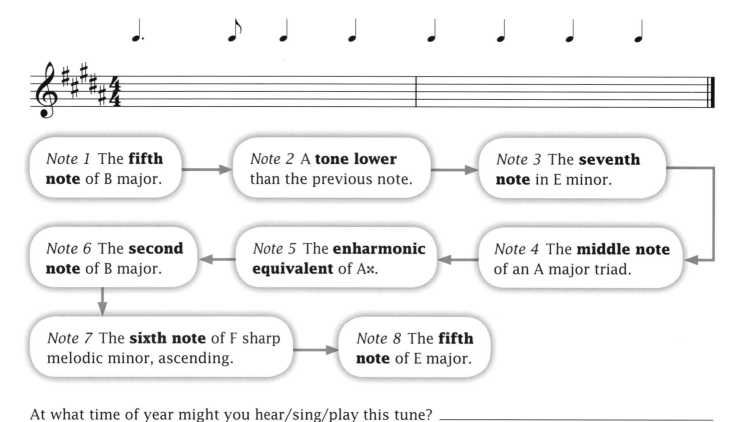

*Note 1* The **fifth note** of B major.

*Note 2* A **tone lower** than the previous note.

*Note 3* The **seventh note** in E minor.

*Note 6* The **second note** of B major.

*Note 5* The **enharmonic equivalent** of A✗.

*Note 4* The **middle note** of an A major triad.

*Note 7* The **sixth note** of F sharp melodic minor, ascending.

*Note 8* The **fifth note** of E major.

At what time of year might you hear/sing/play this tune? _____

**5** Have a look at this piece, then complete the questions below.

### Stop dawdling and be sharpish!

- In which key is this piece? _____ What key is its relative major? _____
- In which bar can you find the notes of the tonic triad? Bar _____
- Write the triad an octave lower and without a key signature:

- What note sounds the same as the first note in bar 4? _____
- Add a double flat or double sharp to the B and G to make them enharmonics equivalents of the A.

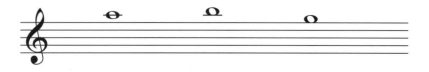

# Making connections to your pieces

Ask your teacher to help you find a piece or song in one of the keys introduced in this stage, and write out the first few bars of the melody on the stave below.

- In what key is the piece? _____     What is its relative key? _____
- Can you find any double sharps or double flats? Circle them in the music.
- Does your piece begin on:   **an upbeat**   **a downbeat**   *(circle)*
- Clap the rhythm and see if you can find any repeated patterns. Write them in the workspace.
- Write out the first two bars in the alto clef in the workspace, either at the same pitch or an octave higher or lower. Did you write it:

   **at the same pitch**   **an octave higher**   **an octave lower**   *(circle)*

### Workspace

# More connections

Write out the first two bars of a piece or song you are learning and notate each note using an enharmonic equivalent – e.g. write F as E♯ or G as F✕. Try your new version out on your teacher or a friend.

# Aural/listening

*(track 4)*

Listen to the following three melodies and decide which:

- is in a major key throughout

   Tune   **1**   **2**   **3**   *(circle)*

- is in a minor key throughout

   Tune   **1**   **2**   **3**   *(circle)*

- uses both major and minor

   Tune   **1**   **2**   **3**   *(circle)*

### Theory box of fun

In the 13th and 14th centuries there were symbols to denote really long notes. The longest was known as the **maxima**, which was *nine times* longer than a breve and *eighteen times* longer than a semibreve! As music developed there became less and less need for notes this long and so they gradually fell into disuse.

# Stage 5

**Facts box** The notes in a scale can be numbered from 1 to 8 to show the **degree** of the scale. For instance, the note D in the scale of C major is 2 as it is the **second degree** of the scale.

Each degree of the scale also has a name:

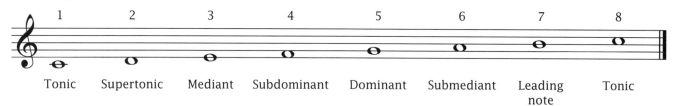

These names apply to both major and minor scales.

**1** Cover up the facts box and then circle whether these statements are true or false.

● The second degree of a scale is called the 'subtonic'.　**true / false**

● The sixth degree of the scale is called the 'submediant'.　**true / false**

● The dominant of G major is C.　**true / false**

**2** What are the degree names of these notes in both the major and minor keys? The first has been completed for you.

i)　　　　　ii)　　　　　iii)

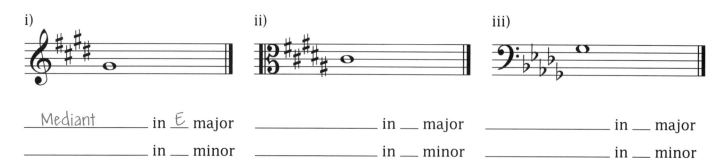

_Mediant_ in E major　\_\_\_\_\_ in \_ major　\_\_\_\_\_ in \_ major
\_\_\_\_\_ in \_ minor　\_\_\_\_\_ in \_ minor　\_\_\_\_\_ in \_ minor

**3** Write out the scale of D melodic minor, descending, giving the degree numbers. Use a key signature.

## Theory box of fun

Why do the majority of scales have 8 notes? Actually it's because of a very complicated and gradual evolution that began with Pythagoras thousands of years ago. The development is actually very scientific and based on the vibrating frequencies of pitches; but the fact is, an 8-note scale sounds good, and makes for tunes that sound like, well … tunes.

**4** Here's a crossword for you to enjoy. It uses some of the words you've recently learned.

ACROSS

2 A pair of two equal notes to be performed in the time of three.

9 To write or play a piece in a different key from the original.

10 The time when you have your ice cream halfway through a play, or the difference between two pitches.

11 The same notes with different names.

12 The spooky sounding minor scale, or the one that's the same going up and coming down.

DOWN

1 A drink that will give you a boost, or the note above the tonic.

3 Lowers a note by two semitones. (6, 4)

4 In any key, the name for the third note of the scale.

5 The clef used by the viola.

6 What you find above the dominant.

7 Happy and optimistic, it comes before the downbeat!

8 A long note; something that you can't do underwater.

**5** Have a look at this piece, then complete the puzzle questions below.

### 'I'll have twelve pieces of eight' said the pirate

**With a sense of evil and menace**

● In what key is the piece? _____

● Put an **X** over all the submediant notes you can find and draw a circle around a dominant.

● Give the meaning of **12/8** _____

● Draw a ⌐‾‾‾¬ over six notes next to each other that form part of the harmonic minor scale.

● What time signature would you use to rewrite this tune with notes of half the value? _____

# Making connections to your pieces

Choose a piece or song you are currently learning and write out
the first few bars on the staves below.

- What is the tonic note of your piece? _____

- On what degree of the scale does your piece begin? _____

- Describe the time signature as simple or compound. _____

- Create a four-bar rhythm using the time signature of your piece. Use the rhythm
  of the first bar to get started. Write it in the workspace and then play or sing
  the rhythm on the following degrees of the piece's key:

  **The dominant      The mediant      The leading note**

Workspace

# More connections

Choose a piece or song you are learning and find an example of all the degrees
of the scale. Tick the box when you've found one:

**tonic** ☐   **supertonic** ☐   **mediant** ☐   **subdominant** ☐   **dominant** ☐

**submediant** ☐   **leading note** ☐

# Aural/listening

In each of these excerpts, you will hear two notes. Can you describe the note
that follows the tonic in each case as supertonic, mediant, subdominant,
dominant, submediant or leading note?

1) _____        2) _____

3) _____        4) _____

# Stage 6

## Facts box

**Triads** can be built on each degree of major and minor scales and they take their name from the degree. For instance:

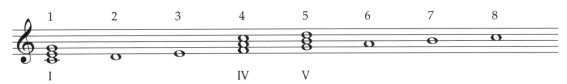

Triads can also be referred to using Roman numerals:
**I (tonic)**, **IV (subdominant)**, **V (dominant)**

**SPECIAL ALERT! Dominant triads in minor keys**
As the middle note of this triad is the 7th degree of the scale, it has to be raised by a semitone in the same way that it is raised when writing or playing the harmonic minor scale. So the dominant triad in minor keys is major!

A **chord** is the name given to two or more notes that are played at the same time.
- Triads are a simple type of chord made up of three notes.
- A tonic triad can also be called a **tonic chord**. However, while the tonic triad always has its notes arranged in the same order (with the tonic at the bottom), the tonic chord can have the notes rearranged into any order:

The same applies to chords built on other degrees of the scale, including the dominant and the subdominant.

**1** Here are the triads built on each degree of the D major scale.
Write I, IV and V under the appropriate triads.

**2** Identify each of these chords by writing I, IV or V next to the given key.

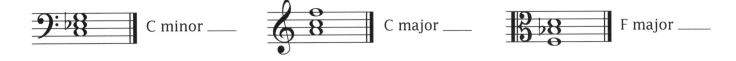

C minor ____    C major ____    F major ____

**3** True or false? The dominant triad of D minor uses the notes A, C and E.    **true / false**

Can you explain your answer? _____

_____

**4** Follow the instructions below and add eight triads, each lasting a minim, to this tune.
The first one has been done for you.

### This tune's a real step up

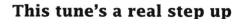

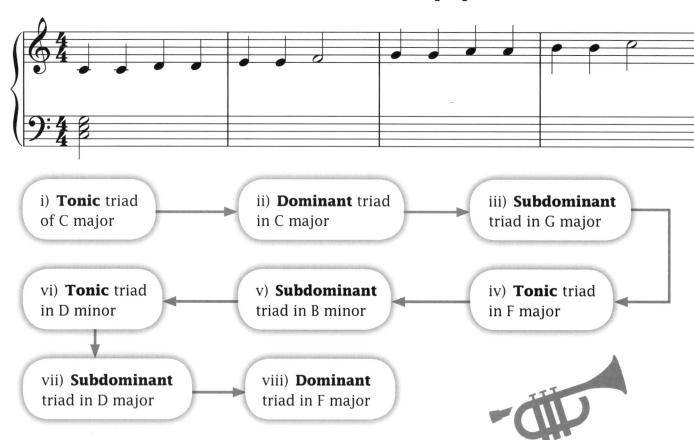

Now play the tune or ask a friend or teacher to play it for you.

**5** Have a look at this fanfare for three trumpets, then complete the puzzle questions below.

### Fanfare: the arrival of the Royal Triad

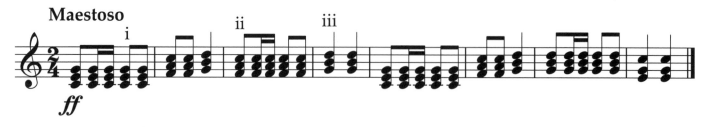

● What is the key of this piece? _____

● Name each of the numbered triads as tonic (I), subdominant (IV) or dominant (V).

i) _____    ii) _____    iii) _____

● The final chord sounds good in performance but is not a tonic
triad. Can you rearrange the notes to make it a tonic triad?

**6** Name the key of this piece and the chords marked with a *
by writing I, IV or V underneath.

### Hymn for Tim

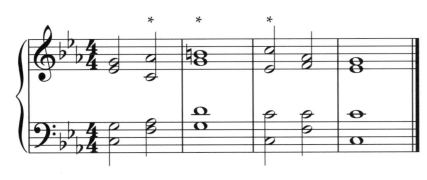

_____  _____  _____                     Key _____

# Making connections to your pieces

Choose a piano piece (or the piano accompaniment to one of your pieces or
songs) that uses chords and/or triads and write out the first few bars on the
staves below. Ask your teacher or a friend to help you find one if you need to.

● In what key is the piece? _____

● Can you find one example of a tonic, subdominant and
dominant chord? If you can, circle them in the music.

# Aural/listening

Listen to the four short pieces and connect the description
with the order they are played.

| A piece containing mostly triads | played 1st |
| A piece with no triads at all | played 2nd |
| A piece with a tune accompanied by triads | played 3rd |
| A piece with big chords | played 4th |

Theory box of fun

The word 'chord' stems from
the Middle English slang
for 'accord', meaning in
agreement or reconciliation.
It began being used in the
16th century to describe a
set of notes that sounded
harmonious when played
together – notes that were
'agreeable' to one another ...
or 'in accord'.

# Stage 7

**Facts box** A **chromatic scale** is a scale that is made up entirely of semitones.

- It can start on any note.
- It contains the same 12 notes but can be written in different ways. For every space and line on the stave, a chromatic scale contains at least one and never more than two notes.

**Enharmonics**
- D♯ and E♭ are the same note (when played on the piano, for example) and are called **enharmonics**.
- Similarly C♯ and D♭, F♯ and G♭, G♯ and A♭, A♯ and B♭ are enharmonic equivalents.
- There are also some slightly more uncommon enharmonics like E♯ and F, B♭♭ and A, F✗ and G.

**1** Add accidentals where needed to make this into a chromatic scale.

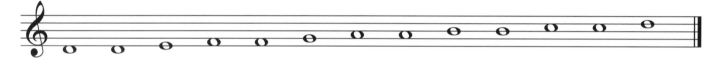

**2** Have a look at this melody and mark any group of four notes that form part of a chromatic scale with a ⌐—⌐.

### A chromatic moment

**3** Label each of these as one of the following:

**chromatic scale    major scale    melodic minor scale**

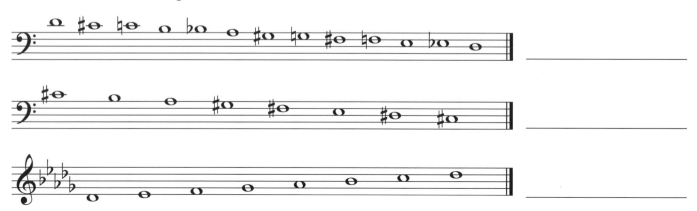

**4** Work your way through the musical statements to reach the chromatic scale. (T = true; F = false)

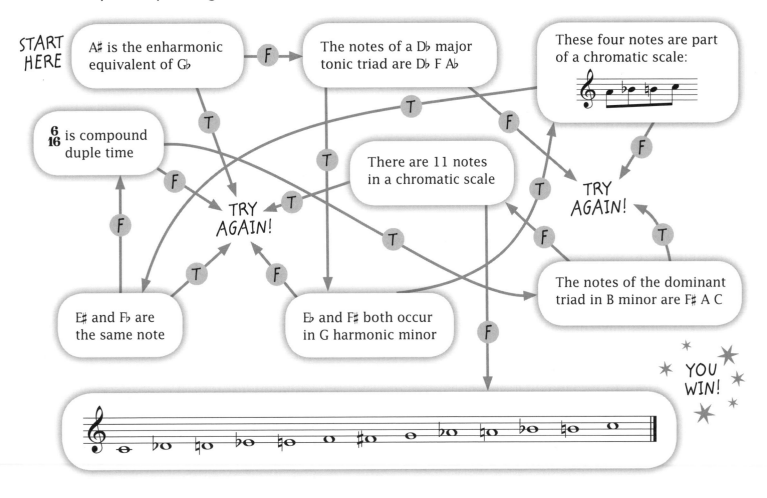

**5** Have a look at this piece, then complete the puzzle questions below.

## All of a quaver

- Find two notes in the piece that are enharmonic equivalents of each other and write them here:

- Add a bracket over the four notes that form a chromatic passage.

- Why are there only three beats in the final bar? _____

- What notes would form the tonic triad of the key of this piece? _____

- Which bars include these notes? _____

# Making connections to your pieces

Find a piece or song you are learning that contains a chromatic sequence and write out a few bars on the staves below. Ask your teacher or a friend to help you find one if you need to.

- How many 'chromatic passages' can you find in your extract? _____
  Mark them with a ⌐─┐ over the music.

- Choose one chromatic passage that you marked and rewrite it in the workspace in the following ways:
  - in a different clef
  - at a different octave
  - writing at least one note in its enharmonic equivalent

 Workspace

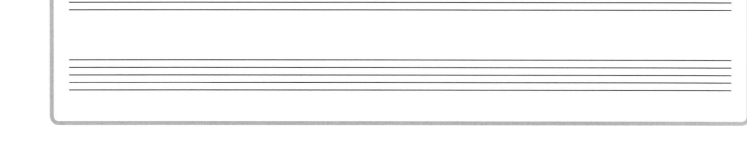

## Aural/listening

Listen to these extracts. Circle the two that contain chromatic passages.

1    2    3

 Theory box of fun

The name for the **chromatic scale** comes from the ancient Greek word 'Chroma' meaning colour, and 'Scala' meaning stairs or ladder – so 'chromatic scale' quite literally means 'colourful ladder'! Play a chromatic scale of your choice, thinking of a different colour for each note.

# Stage 8

**Facts box**

Here are the intervals between all notes within an octave span from C to C:

We're now meeting two new types of interval: **augmented** and **diminished**.

● Increasing a major or perfect interval by a semitone creates an **augmented interval**.

● Decreasing a minor or perfect interval by a semitone creates a **diminished interval**.

| | 2nds | 3rds | 4ths | 5ths | 6ths | 7ths |
|---|---|---|---|---|---|---|
| +1 semi-tone | augmented | augmented | augmented | augmented | augmented | |
| 0 | major | major | perfect | perfect | major | major |
| −1 semi-tone | minor | minor | diminished | diminished | minor | minor |
| −2 semi-tones | | diminished | | | | diminished |

## How to work out an interval

● Look at the lower note. This is note '1' when counting intervals.
● Think of it as a natural (whatever it is) and the first note of a major scale.
● Count up to the upper note. This will give you the interval number.
● Is the upper note in the major scale? If yes, it's a major or perfect interval.
● If no, work out how many semitones smaller or larger than the major-scale interval it is. This will tell you whether it is minor, diminished or augmented.

Here's an example:

● Lower note is F (think F major, ignore the sharp).
● Count from F to E. It's a 7th.
● E is a major 7th above F. E♭ would make it a minor 7th.
● But the F♯ decreases the interval by another semitone, so it's a **diminished 7th**.

**1** Add accidentals to the upper note to create the named harmonic intervals.

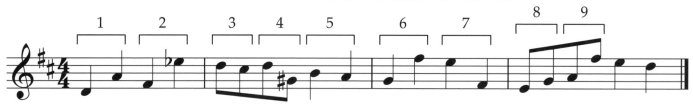

Augmented 2nd    Diminished 5th    Minor 7th    Augmented 4th    Minor 3rd    Major 6th

**2** Have a look at this tune and name the melodic intervals.

### There will now be a 9-minute interval!

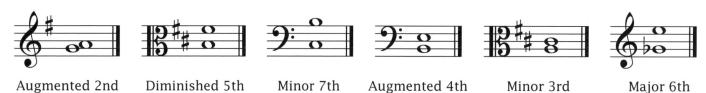

Important Remember that intervals are always counted from the lower note, even if it comes second. Don't forget about the key signature!

1 _____    2 _____    3 _____

4 _____    5 _____    6 _____

7 _____    8 _____    9 _____

**3** Find all of the intervals of a 6th.

- How many of them are major 6ths? _____
- How many are minor 6ths? _____

**4** Have a look at this piece, then complete the questions below.

### Hello mellow fellow! Are you playing the cello?

- Which of the numbered intervals are minor 3rds? _____
- Which bar contains an octave? _____
- What is interval No. 4? _____
- Which bars contain a perfect 4th? _____ and which bars a perfect 5th? _____

# Making connections to your pieces

Find a piece you are learning and write out a few bars on the staves below.

- Does your piece contain:    **melodic intervals?**      **yes / no**    (circle)

                                                      **harmonic intervals?**    **yes / no**    (circle)

- List all of the intervals that you can find in the passage you wrote out.

  _____

  _____

- Choose two different intervals and make up (improvise) your own piece using just those intervals.

# More connections

Rewrite the first two bars in the workspace in the following ways:

i)  at the same pitch but in a different clef

ii) doubling all of the note-values using an appropriate time signature (e.g. ♩ becomes ♪ )

## Workspace

# Aural/listening

Listen to these six intervals and see if you can recognise them:

1 _____        2 _____

3 _____        4 _____

5 _____        6 _____

## Theory box of fun

Alchemists in the 17th century connected the interval of a 7th with the element water, and attributed to it the colours red and orange. They thought that it represented the magical liquid contained within the philosopher's stone that, according to legend, made its owner immortal!

# Stage 9

**Facts box**

### Composing four-bar rhythms from a one-bar opening

- Think about the time signature. How many beats in each bar? What kind of beats?
- If the rhythm begins with an *up-beat* then each phrase will begin on the same beat of the bar (the final beat). Remember to make the first and last bar add up to a complete bar.
- Use similar rhythms for each bar.
- Make the 3rd bar the most exciting (but not too exciting!)
- End on a long note.
- Clap your rhythm (or hear it in your head as you'll have to do in the exam) and feel that it makes *good musical sense*.

### Composing rhythms to words

- All words have rhythm. This is the rhythm of my name:

  Paul Har-ris

  When setting lyrics to a rhythm, say the words aloud and notice the natural accented syllables. This will help you to decide on a time signature. Then circle or underline the accented syllables and add a bar-line before each accented word.
- Make sure that every syllable has a note.
- Add the rhythm above your words, with each syllable placed directly under the note to which it is spoken. Use hyphens to separate syllables within words.
- Begin with a simple rhythm, then see how you can make it a little more imaginative and varied. Here are four different rhythms for 'Cup of tea' in $\frac{3}{4}$ :

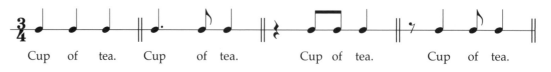

1 Write down the rhythm of your full name on the stave below. Make sure you include a time signature at the start and that the syllables are written under each note.

2 Using the rhythm of your name from question 1, create your own four-bar rhythm and write it on the stave below with a time signature.

Now make up your own words to fit your rhythm.

**3** Clap the one-bar rhythm below and then write down three more bars that are based on it.

Now complete each of these four-bar phrases with related and interesting rhythms.
Have a look at the facts box on page 30 to remind yourself of the 'rules'.

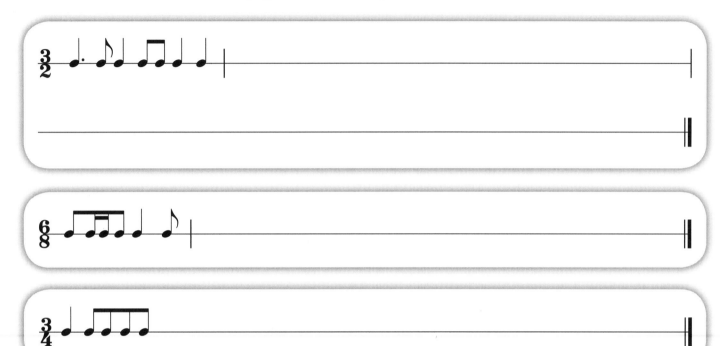

**4** Say these lyrics aloud and then answer the questions below.

> *I love doing theory – it's not a bit dreary.*
> *It's almost as nice as some raspberry ice.*

● Put an accent (>) on the strong syllables.

● Write down any time signatures that would fit the
  rhythm of the words (there may be more than one!) _____

● Think about the mood or character of the words. What kind of rhythm do you
  think would suit this (e.g. bouncy, dotted, slow, repetitive)?

  _____

● Now write the words on the dotted lines and your rhythm on the lines above:

**5** Clap or play the following rhythms and then decide which of the words
   fits best with each one. Write the chosen words under the rhythm.

   1 *The day I did my theory, I'd never been so cheery.*

   2 *Duplets are red but triplets are green; I've always said that theory's a scream!*

   3 *Nothing could be finer than the key of B flat minor.*

i)

ii)

iii)

**6** Here are some more four-bar rhythms for you to complete.

i)

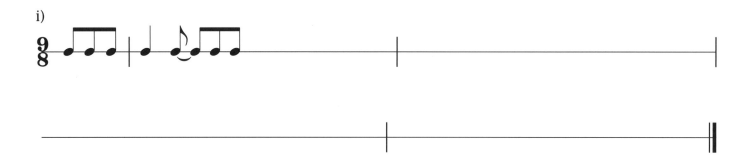

ii)

iii)

**7** Write a four-bar rhythm for the following words.

*Scales are nice like deep fried rice*
*And triads are full of beauty.*
*But chords are just about the best*
*Because they're really fruity.*

**8** Have a look at this piece, then answer the questions below.

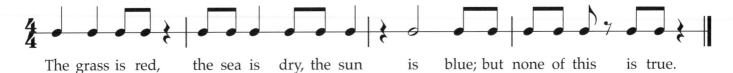

The grass is red,   the sea is   dry, the sun   is   blue; but none of this   is true.

● Is this a good setting of these words? _____

● If you think it's a poor setting, give your reasons here:

_____

_____

Now write your own rhythm to the words:

Theory box of fun

In many African cultures, '**talking drums**' are used as a method of communication. The complex rhythmical sounds are usually made by hand but sometimes with a beater. A skilled player can send messages like, 'Come back home now' or 'Bring some food'. Amazingly the messages can travel up to four or five miles.

# Making connections to your pieces

Find a piece you are learning and choose one bar that has an interesting rhythm. Write the rhythm in bar 1 below:

- Clap or tap the rhythm; how would you describe it (e.g. playful, steady, dotted, repetitive)?

- Add another three bars to make up your own four-bar rhythm.

- Describe how your rhythm compares with the way the original piece develops.

 # More connections

Using your four-bar rhythm:

- rewrite the rhythm in the workspace below, halving or doubling the note-values.
- choose a key and improvise a simple melody to fit your rhythm.
- make up a two- or four-line poem and set it to your rhythm.
- recite your poem.

 Workspace

 # Aural/listening

Listen to these two rhythms and match them up with the words that best fit.

**rhythm 1**      *An apple a day keeps the doctor away.*

**rhythm 2**      *A carpenter is known by his chips.*

# Stage 10

**Facts box**

**Ornaments** are notes that decorate a melody. They are usually written as small notes ('grace notes') or using special signs.

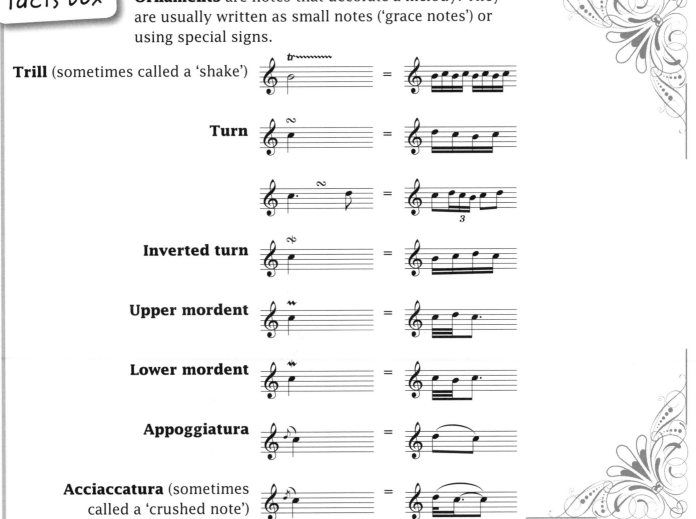

**Trill** (sometimes called a 'shake')

**Turn**

**Inverted turn**

**Upper mordent**

**Lower mordent**

**Appoggiatura**

**Acciaccatura** (sometimes called a 'crushed note')

**1** Identify each numbered ornament and then try to play this melody or ask your teacher to play it for you.

i) _____   ii) _____   iii) _____

iv) _____   v) _____

**2** Identify each of these written-out ornaments:

**3** Enjoy this crossword. All the answers are types of ornaments.

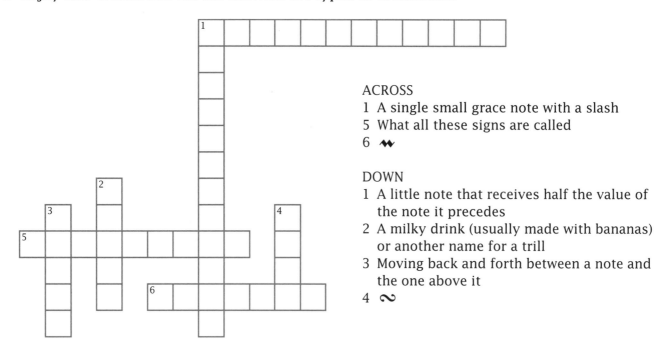

ACROSS
1 A single small grace note with a slash
5 What all these signs are called
6 ♦♦

DOWN
1 A little note that receives half the value of the note it precedes
2 A milky drink (usually made with bananas) or another name for a trill
3 Moving back and forth between a note and the one above it
4 ∽

**4** Have a look at this piece, then complete the puzzle questions below.

### How very ornamental!

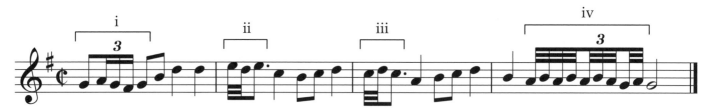

● Write out the notes under each bracket as an ornament, using the correct symbols, and name each one.

i) ▭ Ornament: _____

ii) ▭ Ornament: _____

iii) ▭ Ornament: _____

iv) ▭ Ornament: _____

● What is the key? _____

● Try to play the tune or ask your teacher or a friend to play it to you.

# Making connections to your pieces

Find a piece you are learning that contains some ornaments. Ask your teacher to find you an example if you don't have one. Write out a few bars of the melody line on the staves below.

- How many different kinds of ornamentation can you find? _____

  Circle them in the music and write their names underneath.

- Find out the name of the musical period when ornaments were extremely common and name some composers who lived and worked in that period. Write your findings in the workspace.

 Workspace

# More connections

Make up (improvise) your own piece in the same key, using some ornamentation. Which ornaments did you use?

_____

# Aural/listening

**track 10**

You will hear four extracts, each containing one kind of ornamentation. Match up the extract with the ornamentation used.

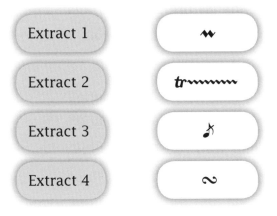

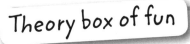

## Theory box of fun

For three whole centuries, from 1600 until 1900, the **appoggiatura** was the most widespread ornament used in music. In opera it was the way to indicate dramatic sobs, when the character singing is crying or having a tantrum!

# Stage 11

 **Facts box** Instruments can be grouped into different 'families', depending on the material they are made from and how they produce the sound.

### Woodwind

- Produce sound by a column of air vibrating within a hollow tube
- 𝄞 **piccolo**, **flute**, **oboe**, **clarinet**, **cor anglais**, **saxophone**
- 𝄢 **bassoon**

### Keyboards

- Instruments with keys that are depressed to produce different pitches
- **pianoforte (piano)**, **harpsichord**, **organ**

### Brass

- Produce sound by a column of air vibrating within a hollow tube
- 𝄞 **French horn**, **trumpet**
- 𝄢 **trombone**, **tuba**

### Strings

- Made of wood
- Produce sound by plucking or drawing a bow across the strings
- 𝄞 **violin**
- 𝄡 **viola**
- 𝄢 **cello**, **double bass**

### Percussion

- Pitched and unpitched instruments that produce sound by being struck
- ╟─── unpitched: **side drum**, **tambourine**, **cymbal**, **gong**
- 𝄞 pitched: **glockenspiel**, **xylophone**, **tubular bells**
- 𝄢 pitched: **timpani**

### Performance directions for instruments

| | | |
|---|---|---|
| *con sordino (con sord.)* | play with mute | (strings and brass) |
| *senza sordino (senza sord.)* | play without mute | (strings and brass) |
| *pizzicato (pizz.)* | pluck the string | (strings) |
| *arco* | play with the bow | (strings) |
| ⊓  ⋁ | 'down' bow, 'up' bow | (strings) |
| *col legno* | play with the bow upside-down | (strings) |
| *sul G, sul ponticello* | play on the G string, play near the bridge | (strings) |
| *con pedal (con Ped.)* | play with the sustaining pedal | (piano) |
| 𝄢𝄔._____ | | |
| ⁞ | spread the notes of a chord quickly from the bottom upwards | (piano) |
| *una corda, tre corde* | press the left pedal, press the right pedal | (piano) |
| *mano sinistra (m.s.),* | left hand, | (piano) |
| *mano destra (m.d.)* | right hand | |

See page 48 for more performance directions.

**1** The piccolo is the highest sounding woodwind instrument, sounding
one octave higher than the notes are written. Rewrite this piccolo
melody up one octave at its sounding pitch.

**Flying high**

**2** The double bass is the lowest sounding orchestral string instrument, sounding
one octave lower than the notes are written. Rewrite this double-bass melody
at its sounding pitch.

**Deep down**

**3** Rewrite this passage in the alto clef, keeping the pitches the same.

**The King of Clubs and the Queen of Hearts have a cup of tea**

Name one instrument that might
play this melody in the treble clef
and one that might play it in the
alto clef.

Treble clef  _____

Alto clef  _____

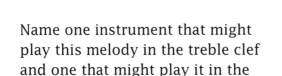

Breaking the world record in 1998, the largest (and
loudest!) children's orchestra assembled at the National
Arena in Birmingham to play Malcolm Arnold's *Little
Suite No.2*. There were 3,889 musicians: 1600 strings, 1300
woodwind, 800 brass and over 200 percussion players!

**4** Circle the instruments listed below that are *unpitched*.

**triangle    piano    snare drum    trombone    cymbal    glockenspiel**    *(circle)*

**5** Select the most appropriate instrument for each of these extracts.

**viola    wood block    trumpet**

i)    **Presto**

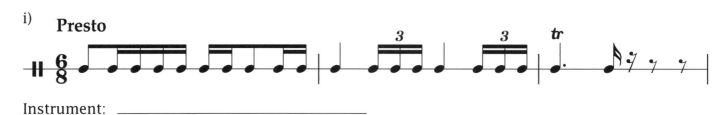

Instrument: _____

ii)    **Maestoso**

Instrument: _____

iii)    **Vif**

Instrument: _____

**6** Have a look at this piece, then complete the puzzle questions below.

**Mint chocolate minuet**

● What does *Modéré et douce* mean? _____

● Which instrument do you think this melody is written for?

**clarinet    piano    triangle    cello    trumpet    piccolo    violin**    *(circle)*

● Name the symbol used in bar 2 and describe its meaning. _____

_____

# Making connections to your pieces

Write out a few bars of a piece that you like playing on the staves below.

Fill each of these bubbles with an interesting feature from your piece.

| rhythm | patterns | character |
|---|---|---|

| performance directions | melody | key |
|---|---|---|

# More connections

Find out something about the history of your instrument. When did it first appear? Was it invented? Who wrote the first music for it? If you are a singer, find out when the first notated songs were written and who wrote them. Write your findings in the workspace.

**Workspace**

# Aural/listening

track 11

Match up these extracts with the correct instrument and instrument family.

| Extract 1 | organ | brass |
| Extract 2 | cello (plucked) | strings |
| Extract 3 | piccolo | keyboard |
| Extract 4 | trumpet | woodwind |

# Stage 12

**1** Insert the correct time signatures at the start of these rhythms.

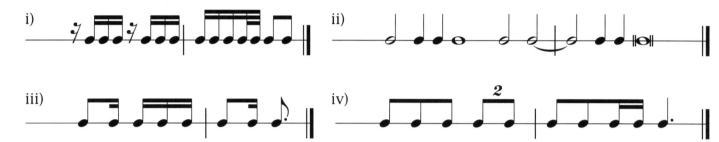

**2** Rewrite this rhythm with the notes and rests correctly grouped.

**3** Add the correct rests at the * to complete this tune.

**4** Rewrite this tune in the ways described below.
Remember to include the new time signature.

**I think I have A FLAT tyre**

i) Using notes of *half* the value.

ii) In simple time, without changing the rhythmic effect.

**5** Create your own four-bar rhythm in a time signature of your
choice and write it on the stave below.

**6** Make up your own rhythm to fit these words.

> *I love eating mango when dancing the tango.*
> *But nothing beats courgette when playing a minuet.*

**7** Name the notes marked with a *.

### Passion fruit and banana milkshake, please

**8** Rewrite this tune in the following ways:

### Un petit rose rouge croissante dans le grand jardin

i) at the same pitch but in the alto clef.

ii) one octave higher in the treble clef.

**9** Write out the scale of B♭ melodic minor (ascending) in breves,
using the alto clef. Use accidentals instead of a key signature.

**10** Identify these tonic triads by writing I, IV, V underneath. The first one has been given.

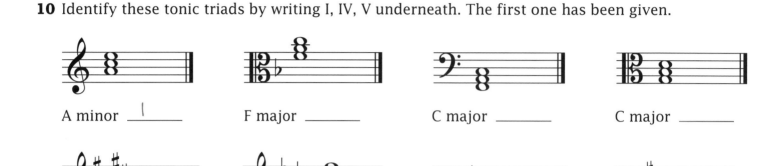

A minor __I__          F major _____          C major _____          C major _____

C♯ minor _____          B♭ minor _____          F minor _____          D major _____

**11** Write out the scale of G♯ melodic minor (descending) in crotchets and using the bass
clef. Give the degree names and numbers under each note. Use a key signature.

**12** Rewrite each of these notes as an enharmonic equivalent.

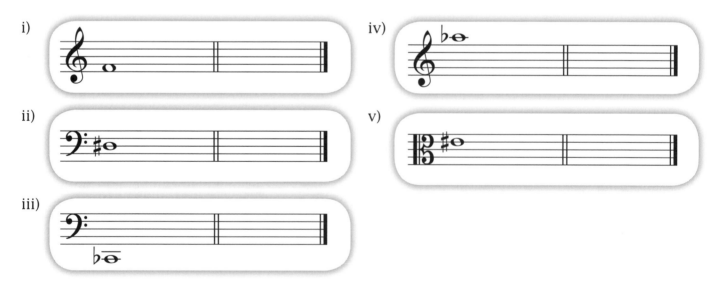

**13** Write triads as indicated below each stave using accidentals but no key signature.

G♭ major   V                    E minor   IV                    A♭ major   I                    C♯ minor   V

**14** Name each of the chords marked with a * as tonic (I), subdominant (IV) or dominant (V).

### B careful ... Bs about!

In what key is this piece? _____

**15** Add notes after those given to create the named melodic intervals.

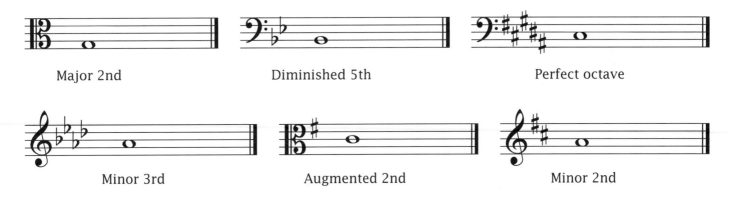

Major 2nd                    Diminished 5th                    Perfect octave

Minor 3rd                    Augmented 2nd                    Minor 2nd

**16** Write out a chromatic scale starting on the note B, in the alto clef in semibreves.

**17** Name the following ornaments.

_____        _____        _____

**18** Name a standard orchestral instrument that fits each of these descriptions.

i) A string instrument that usually uses the treble clef _____

ii) A woodwind instrument that sounds one octave higher than it is written _____

iii) The lowest sounding member of the string family _____

iv) An instrument that might be played *con sordino* _____

v) An unpitched percussion instrument _____

**19** Study this piece and then answer the questions below.

### Rush hour!

- Add the correct time signature at the start of the piece.

- In what key is the piece? _____

- Give the meaning of the following words and signs:

    i)   *Allegro con fuoco* _____

    ii)  ♩. = 96 _____

    iii) > _____

- Draw a ⌐‾⌐ over the 11 notes that form part of a chromatic scale.

- Write the enharmonic equivalent of the 1st note in bar 2 (*) as a breve:

- Describe in full the melodic intervals labelled *i, ii* and *iii* in this extract
  (e.g. 'minor 3rd').

    i) _____   ii) _____   iii) _____

- Transpose the melody of bar 3 down one octave and write it in the bass clef.

- Name the ornament used on the 1st beat of bar 1. _____

- Give the degree name of the first note in bar 2 (e.g. 'tonic'). _____

- What is the relative key? _____

- Which of the following instruments might this piece be played on?

    **flute    violin    bassoon    trumpet    clarinet    viola**    *(circle the most suitable)*

**20** How many signs and symbols can you find in Theory Robot?

Write them here

Congratulations

on completing **Improve your theory! Grade 4.**
See you again for Grade 5!

# Appendix

## More performance markings

### Italian

*affettuoso* tenderly
*affrettando* hurrying
*calando* getting softer
*cantando* singing style
*facile* easy
*fuoco* fire
*tempo giusto* strict time
*l'istesso tempo* at the same speed
*morendo* dying away
*niente* nothing
*nobilmente* noble
*perdendosi* dying away
*possibile* possible
*quasi* as if
*sonoro* sonorous
*sotto voce* in an undertone
*veloce* swift

### French

*animé* animated
*assez* enough
*avec, sans* with, without
*cédez* yield, slow down
*douce* sweet
*en dehors* prominent
*en pressant* hurrying on
*légèrement* light
*lent* slow
*mais* but
*modéré* moderate speed
*peu, plus, moins* little, more, less
*ralentir* getting slower
*retenu* held back
*très* very
*vif* lively
*vite* quick

© 2015 by Faber Music Ltd
Bloomsbury House
74–77 Great Russell Street
London
WC1B 3DA

Music setting by Donald Thomson
Cover and page design by Susan Clarke
Illustrations from Thinkstockphotos.co.uk
Audio tracks recorded and produced by Oliver Wedgwood,
 performed by Paul Harris
Printed in England by Caligraving Ltd
All rights reserved

ISBN10: 0-571-53864-9
EAN13: 978-0-571-53864-5

To buy Faber Music publications or to find out about the full range of titles available
please contact your local music retailer or Faber Music sales enquiries:
Faber Music Ltd, Burnt Mill, Elizabeth Way, Harlow CM20 2HX
Tel: +44 (0) 1279 82 89 82   Fax: 44 (0) 1279 82 89 83
sales@fabermusic.com   fabermusicstore.com